Inspired
2
Inspire

C.D Walker

This book is dedicated to my lovely wife of 19 years, Angela Walker and our beautiful children LeAsia and CJ.

Hello friend

I pray this book inspire you to do things that you would have never done. I have compiled 52 of my favorite empowerment quotes from some powerful and influential people as well as my own. I hope you find these quotes to be as inspiring as I did.

Your Friend and brother,
C. D. Walker

Empowerment 1

"When God says "leave," don't linger. It's His responsibility to give you instructions and it's your responsibility to follow them"

-Noel Jones

Often times we linger in the place that God has told us to leave. We must not be sessile to a situation or a circumstance that causes us not to obey the voice of God. We pray and God deliver us and we turn right around and fight to stay in the very thing we want out of. We must trust God to guide us in the unknown and that which is unfamiliar. We tend to stay in a place that is not good for us because it is comfortable. Let go and trust God so you can walk into your place He has predestined for you.

Empowerment 2

"God maneuvers you into a position of influence so you can effectively change situations for others who have a lesser degree of favor."

-T.D. Jakes

God has graced you for the position that you are in, your influence is connected to the favor of God that is on your life. You are in the position to make whatever environment you are in better. Build people up who have lost all hope and think that all is lost. Submit to God like Joseph and go through so you can help get others through whatever famine they are facing.

Read Genesis Chapters 37-45

Empowerment 3

"Vision is like a scratch on your glasses, you see the flaw as soon as you put them on, but the longer you wear them, the more you focus on things down the road, instead of what is in front of you."

C.D. Walker

Things that are present in your life will try to take priority over the vision that God has given you. You have made a lot of bad decisions, mistakes and missed opportunities, but it does not mean that the vision is unattainable; I wear my issues every day, no I'm not perfect, yes I have made mistakes and probably will make more, but I refuse to allow those things to cloud my vision. Be clear where you are going but also be prepared for traffic jams, flat tires and detours in this life. Do not let that stop you from getting to your destination.

Empowerment 4

"Stick with the plan! One of Satan's greatest tactics is diverting our attention elsewhere before we've completed our assignment."

-Bishop M Moore

God gave you an assignment with a plan. He knew your adversary; the devil would try to divert your attention somewhere else. Jesus came to earth with a plan, and that was to be the ultimate sacrifice, and the enemy tried to divert him away from the cross by telling him to come down. But Jesus completed His assignment and said "It is finished". Jesus rose with all power of the adversary and has left us to be ruler over the devil. Complete you assignment!

Read Hebrew 12:2

Empowerment 5

Every believer lives in the tension between the promise and reality.

-Lance Watson

We all have said, Lord I believe, but. We believe but the unbelief that is present as well, is trying to overcome what we have told ourselves we believe. We must get into a place that we are settled and confident with God. With man it is impossible, but with God nothing is impossible. Stop trying to figure it out. I know it seems like you have been dealing with this forever and your belief is on its last leg. Know that God has promise in your life, He will do.

Read Mark 9:17-24

Empowerment 6

Don't be star struck by the bait, and get yourself hooked emotionally and hate what's on the other end of the line.

-C.D. Walker

We all have used bait and we all have been hooked. Quit baiting people with false intentions. Be honest up front, because the real you will eventually show up. Bait is nothing more than a lure of something that is already dead, dying, or that is not real. Stop getting hooked and learn to discern the spirit behind everything.

Empowerment 7

We all have the ability to change someone's life
-Antoine de Saint Exupery

Change is inevitable. It is when you make a conscience decision to make a difference in someone else's life that you can grow in areas unknown. You might be saying, how can I change someone's life? It is really simple, tell someone good morning, pay for someone else lunch, buy groceries for someone, mentor a youth, invite someone to church or just a simple smile. You have the ability to change the outcome of a person's day by being kind. What are you waiting on SMILE.

Empowerment 8

"A goal without a plan is just a wish"

-C.D. Walker

Goal is defined as: The results or achievement toward which effort is directed; aim; end.

Most people set goals and become less, because they did not count the cost. They did not realize the effort that it would take to obtain the set goal. It required more effort than they were willing to exert. Often times people set goals and the end results is someone else effort. Do your homework, make it attainable and don't over think it. Set a time for completing your goal and work your plan with effort and self-motivation.

Empowerment 9

"Excellence is the unlimited ability to improve the quality of what you have to offer."

-Rick Pitino

We offer people something every day. The question to ask is, "I am offering the best I can offer". Some of you may think that you do not have anything to offer anyone, but you do. We all have talents, knowledge, and experience that we can offer. Whatever we do, we need to make sure that we are doing the very best that we can. Operating in the spirit of Excellency will raise others expectations and cause them to do their best. Remember, whatever you do, do it as unto the Lord. We should always give Him our best.

Empowerment 10

*Until you make peace with who you are, you'll
never be content with what you have*
                                         -Doris Mortman

Being who we really are is one of the
greatest struggles we face. We cannot
make peace with somebody we do not
know. Everybody is not a movie star, pop
singer, American idol, millionaire, Atlanta
house wife, or business owner. You might
be a stocker at Wal-Mart, drive thru
worker at McDonalds, cashier, etc.....
Regardless of what job you do, do not
lose your ambition and drive to reaching
your full potential. Learn to be happy
about who you are at this present state
but continue to become who God want
you to be. Read Philippians 4: 11-14

Empowerment 11

"Efforts and courage are not enough without purpose and direction."

-John F. Kennedy

Understanding your purpose will give you direction. Growing up in life we have wasted a lot of effort and had courage in wrong things. We should no longer be children tossed to and fro, but grounded and fixated on our purpose. We must live life intentional, not just what comes our way. We go through life asking, "What is my purpose", but we fail to ask the very one that know, God. He has put purpose in every one of us, and He will be the one that will show us what to do.

Read Jeremiah 29: 11-13

Empowerment 12

"Not everything that is faced can be changed, but nothing can be changed until it is faced."

-James Baldwin

We all have experienced situations that seemed unfair. We have told ourselves that "no one will listen" or "how can I make a difference" or "let someone else speak up". Most of the time things never change because everyone has followed suit and never stepped up to the plate. People are naturally selfish, so we will make decisions based on our situations and needs and do not think about how our decisions affect others. Let us learn how to face the things in life we are faced with instead of not speaking up or making selfish decisions.

Empowerment 13

"Being chosen doesn't exempt you from challenges; being anointed will not abbreviate your adversities"

-Lance Watson

To whom much is given, much is required. When you understand that you were chosen by God, you understand your position. Then will you will understand the dynamics of the position. Your response to adversity will be different. Submitting to the will of God will set you apart from the rest. When you are chosen, whatever comes your way, God will see you through it.

Read Romans 8:28-30

Empowerment 14

"You will do what you know until you know how to do better."

-Cindy Trimm

In life you will do things your way and it will only take you so far. The longer you do things your way, the more it becomes your reality. You make decisions based on the information that you have at that time. Allow yourself to submit to wise counsel (people that will challenge your decision making). Do not get offended when someone tells you that you are wrong. If you think you are always right, no one can help you. Your life will change as you change your way of thinking.

Empowerment 15

"Don't use prayer and faith as a parachute expecting God to save you after you've done your stunts!"

-Bishop C. Blake

Often times we have plotted and schemed when were up to no good, somewhere we shouldn't be doing something we know we shouldn't. We have even said the pray, Lord I know this is wrong….. Stop right there! So we pray to do wrong and expect God to cover us! We cannot expect God to bless us in our mess. Instead, we should pray and ask God to help us fight the temptation that we are facing at that moment. Temptation is going to come as long as we are in this flesh, but we do not have to be overtaken. We have help! Resist the devil and he has to flee!

Read Romans 6: 1-2

Empowerment 16

"The attack right now has nothing to do with who you are, but who you are going to become."
-Bishop Bloomer

When you are called by God, you are on an assignment. The attack is not about you, it is against the assignment. The only person that can abort the assignment is you. The enemy understands that, so he attacks you so that you become discouraged in such a way that you begin to doubt yourself, your assignment and God. Be strong and know that God has equipped you for the task.

Read 2 Timothy 2: 1-4

Empowerment 17

"Your deliverance does not make you a judge, understanding what it took for you to be delivered should cause you to be a compassionate specialist."

-C.D. Walker

It is amazing to me that we forget where God has brought us from. God saved us, cleaned us up, and expected us right where we were. Now that we think we are somebody, we decide to judge everybody else that is doing the very things we use to do. God did not deliver you so that you can become a judge, but a light to a dying world. We must exemplify Christ in our lives. We are commanded to love one another even with our differences and disagreements. Love does not judge.

Read 1 Corinthians 13: 4-7

Empowerment 18

"Insecure leaders try to lead by control. Confident leaders inspire & release"
-Brian Houston

Leadership is not control. Leadership is when you are able to see the gift/talent in those you lead and nurture it so it will reach its full potential. Most leaders become insecure and jealous of others gifts. Instead to using the follower's gifts as an asset to the team, some leaders try to undermine and intimidate the people of God. Your gifts will make room for you. You do not need anyone to validate your gift. Leaders learn to release the gifts that God has placed in your mist. They are there for a reason.

Empowerment 19

Love is one of the greatest gifts we have available to us. We can give it and we can receive it. But what is love? What does it look like? Have we confused love with something else? Until we discover true love, the very thing that we associate with love with will eventually let you down. Love begins with God, because He is Love. You will not truly know how to love until you know get to know God on a personal level and not just hearing about Him.

Empowerment 20

"You can never cross the ocean unless you have the courage to lose sight of the shore."
                                    -Christopher Columbus

One of the things that will hinder you from moving is the fear of the unknown. You will never be able to cross the ocean because you are not solidified your reason for crossing, you have not prepared for the journey or you are not strong enough to withstand the waves and storms that will come. Your passion to stay on the shore has not created a urgency in you to cross. Set a launch date, prepare and set sail. Your blessings are on the other side waiting on you!

Empowerment 21

"You never really understand a person until you consider things from his point of view"

-Harper Lee

We have all heard the saying. "Don't judge a book by its cover". It is easy to judge or give your opinion on something that you do not understand. Most people do thing according to their culture, religion, or upbringing. Not everybody think the same. We lack so many opportunities to connect with people from different cultures because we refuse to see things from their point of view. We must get out of the mindset that our view is the only view of things. We must be more understanding than judgmental.

Empowerment 22

"No pressure, no diamonds"

-Mary Case

A diamond does not start out a diamond, but a piece of coal. We always see the end results and not the process. Unless the coal goes through the process of being under tremendous pressure, it will always remain a lump of coal. Sometime you never know what you are capable of until you are under pressure. God allow situations to take place in your life to reveal the gift that He has placed in the inside of you. Remember, no pressure, no diamond.

Empowerment 23

"Often we are frustrated in life because we're waiting on God to do what God is waiting on us to do."

-Lance Watson

Life deals with a lot of decisions we make every day. For instance, every morning you have to make a decision to get out of bed and go to work or school. As simple as that is, you made a decision that affected not only you but your entire family. I have found myself frustrated because I knew God had place purpose on my life and given me a vision but I was waiting on God to move. I was trying to be so careful not to move ahead of God, that I was unable to sense that God had already released me to do what he called to do. God is speaking, be in position to here and move when He says move.

Empowerment 24

"I must do something" will always solve more problems than "Something must be done"
-Lance Watson

People always complain about things and say somebody should do something about this or that, but they never volunteer to make a difference. "Those children are bad", then you should become a mentor to them. "My job is terrible", become supervisor and implement change. Become the difference maker to situations instead of complaining about it. Take responsibility and build a team of problem solvers, and stop being a part of the problem. Become the change you want to see.

Empowerment 25

"The road to mastery passes through the valley of mistakes, but we must remember to never stay in the valley"

-I.V. Hilliard

Mistakes are a part of life, especially when you are striving for perfection. You cannot become a master of anything unless you travel through the valley of mistakes. I view mistakes as a lesson. They get harder until the lesson is learned. How will you know you have learned from your mistakes? When you say, I will never do that again! Sometimes you have to deal with consequences for your mistakes. Do not allow your mistakes to keep you in the valley. You must reach the mountain top. Acknowledge your mistakes, learn from it and move on.

Empowerment 26

"God cannot bring His will to pass in your life without your permission and participation"
-Bishop Hilliard

God is all powerful, but he does not make us participate in the plan that he has for us, why because he has given us free will. Free will is an independent choice; voluntary decision. In order for the thing that is created to fulfill its purpose, it must submit and participate with the creator's design. In order for you to receive the full benefits of God's blessing you have to follow the instruction that God gives you. The first thing any believer must have is Faith, without faith it is impossible to please God. God will never bomb rush your life, you must ask him to come in.

Empowerment 27

"Sometime you make the right decision and sometime you have to make the decision right."

-C.D. Walker

How many times have you made a good decision, well you thought it was in the beginning and it seemed to be the right one at the time, but as time went on you've noticed that the decision you made worked and was relevant, but now you need to make an adjustment, because you are in a different place then you were back then. Now you have to make that decision right, by choosing to close the term of that decision. Most people feel that once they make a decision, they have to stick with it even though you know it's not working out, but in order to save face, keeping your image intact and worrying about what people will say about you, you stick/die with the decision you made. All decisions are not the right ones, but once you realize it, change.

Empowerment 28

Whenever you embark on a new marriage/relationship/job/friendship, coming together is the beginning of something special, but be aware of the difficult moments that will challenge you, issue that will arise that will cause you to feel a little reluctant about the relationship. I believe the reason most relationships fail is because of the expectation that we put on the other person, and that expectation is perfection. We all are human and we make mistakes. Everybody has an opinion and they are entitled to it and you have to respect it. Keeping the relationship together is a process, which means that I am able to see your faults and still love you. Talking through your issues with each other goes a long way, and most of the time it is just our own pride standing in the way. Communication is the key to the success of any relationship.

Empowerment 29

"Even when your life is falling apart, God is collecting the pieces preparing to put it back together"

-Lance Watson

If you have lived any length of time, you have experienced your life falling apart to some degree. Have you ever experienced a day when you got a speeding ticket, flat tire, traffic jam, disconnection notice, lights cutoff, vehicle repossessed, fired from your job, lost a love one, served divorce papers, diagnosed with cancer, had a miscarriage, cheated on, burglarized, abused, missed an appointment, wages garnished etc…. Even then your life is not over, even though it does not feel good, but God is able to keep you from losing your mind, even when you putting on that fake facade that everything is ok, but on the inside you are at the edge. Once the dust settles and you gather your bearing, then you began to sense God's hand in your life putting you back together, even when you thought you were beyond repair. Even when you fall God is right there to catch you.

Empowerment 30

"The only reason the devil is trying to kill me is not because of my problem it is because of my potential"

-Unknown

The devil is always trying to take our potential, for example, Moses and Jesus. The enemy understood Moses potential and what God promised the children of Israel, that he would deliver them, even though it had been 400 years. The deliver was born, Moses, but God protected Moses, as well as his potential/purpose. Jesus the ultimate deliver/Lamb of God that would take away the sins of the entire world, robed in flesh came on the scene and the enemy was very persistent in taking him out even as a baby, but God has a plan and a purpose. Realize your potential and bring chaos to the kingdom of darkness.

Empowerment 31

"It's not what you are that holds you back, it's what you think you are not."

-Denis Waitley

There is an old song that goes like this "I am standing to close to the mirror to see what you see". My whole life I knew that there was always more for me than what I had and where I was, but I often settled for where I was and what I was doing at the time, but the gift on the inside, that I never recognized at the time, would rise up in me and cause me to hunger for more, but I would just suppress the unction and try to ignore it, but it never went away, and I never had any peace. Once the gift was unleashed I had and still struggle with what God says I am and me telling myself I am not worthy and why me. I am in and out of what God says that I am. I am David Banner more than I am the Incredible Hulk, but when I am the Hulk I am in my purpose, but my doubts about myself tends to hold me back. Abraham was called the father of many nations before he had kids. It's amazing how we believe and allow what other people call us or say about us, but do not believe what God told us that we will be. Tell yourself that I am everything that God says that I am.

Empowerment 32

*"You cannot leave your happiness up to someone
else."*

-C.D. Walker

The world is full of miserable people, because
they have conditioned themselves into thinking
that money, things or people are responsible for
their happiness. News flash, nobody is
responsible for your happiness, but you. I have
been married for almost 20 years and I told my
wife that I am not responsible for her happiness,
but I make her happy, but her happiness solely
depends on her and vice versa. Quit holding
people hostage because you are not happy, that's
not their responsibility. Happiness is a choice
and a state of mind. You can choose to be happy
even when all hell is breaking loose in your life.
The songwriter stated that the joy of the Lord is
his strength. Take joy in knowing that it's
already done, and you've already won, because
Jesus made it possible.

Empowerment 33

"The stronger the anointing within you, the greater the responsibility of that anointing upon you!"

-Benny Hinn

In order to do what God has called you to do, he has to place an anointing upon you that you will be able to fulfill your mission, of destroying the yokes, setting the captive free and the tearing down of strong holds. The greater the purpose, the greater the anointing that it will take to fulfill your mission. God has graced you for the mission. Know that everything you need God has already given to you. You win!

Empowerment 34

"The ability to simplify means to eliminate the unnecessary, so the necessary can glow."

-Cindy Trimm

We try to compact so much in 24 hours that we have been given, and it appears that we need more time, but the truth of the matter is that we need to simplify our lives and get rid of the dead weight and the things that have taken us hostage, and I know one of the main enemies, and that is procrastination. Procrastination will lead you to believe that you have time and you can do it later, that which needs to be done now. You must prune the things that serve no purpose in your life. We have become hoarders of things that are not connected to our destiny. Evaluate your life and get rid of stuff that has been holding you down for years, so the necessary stuff can glow. It's necessary to eliminate the unnecessary in your life.

Empowerment 35

"Until you make peace with who you are, you'll never be content with what you have."

-Doris Mortman

So many people are defined by what they have, and have not truly understood, nor discovered who they really are. I have chase things that were not meant for me to have, even though I attained it. There are two important days in your life, the day you were born and the day you understand why. So many of us chase things and yet we never attain it and we are left feeling empty and discouraged. When you understand who your, you can be content with what you have, and most of the things you have, you will want to give up, because you will rather lose everything in order to obtain Christ. Read Philippians 3:7-12.

Empowerment 36

"Nothing will ever be attempted if you do not overcome negative opinions."

-C.D. Walker

Anytime you go to do something, negativity is ready to pounce on you, to beat you up and make you believe that you cannot accomplish that which you have set your mind to do. You do not have time to deal will with and address every negative opinion that arises. Use the negative things as stepping stones and rise to the occasion, because if you stop to deal with the negative stuff you will never get where you are trying to go. Negativity will cause you to get into a debate of why you cannot do something, but instead respond to negativity by doing what you set out to do. Finishing will close the mouth of negativity.

Empowerment 37

"Snowflakes are one of nature's most fragile things, but just look at what they can do when they stick together."

-Vesta Kelly

No matter how small a thing is or how fragile, we can all learn from the snowflake. Under the right conditions can bring a blizzard that can cripple a city and bring it to its knees. We all need to learn to stick together and put our own agendas to the side and look at the big picture, but instead we as individuals just want to be big. One snowflake is insignificant, but a whole lot of snowflake can make an impact. Look for people that you can band together with and make a difference.

Empowerment 38

"Love is action and not just words"

-C.D. Walker

Love is an action word, and is meaningless without action. Love is shown more than it is spoken, but action not in the act of love is irrelevant, if you act out of love, that means you had that person in mind before you ever made a move. You carefully considered the effect it would have on the other person. Love is putting others before yourself, even at times when they do not deserve it, but know this, we have all been that undeserving individual.

Empowerment 39

"Progress is impossible without change and those who cannot change their minds cannot change anything."
-C.D. Walker

Have you ever wondered why you were not making any progress, even though you were giving it your all? Hard work alone does not guarantee progress. Hard work is going to deal with the change that has to take place in your life in order to make progress. It's like cutting a tree with a dull ax, you have big muscles, you are swinging hard and striking the tree in the same spot, but you are getting no closer to cutting the tree down, until you sharpened(change) the ax, and you might have to sharpen it several times during the process. Adjustments are a part of the process. Unless you change, you will remain the same.

Empowerment 40

"Forgiveness is a beautiful word when you need it, but it's a painful word when you have to give it. Grow and Go."

-Kirk Franklin

We plead and beg for someone to forgive us when mess up, and we are so grateful for the grace, but when it is our time to forgive someone else, it becomes grievous to us and we forget the favor that was shown toward us, because we are caught up emotionally with what that person did to us and they should pay for their mistake. Forgiveness is easier to ask for than it is to give. God demands it from each and every last one of us.   Love your enemies, pray for those who despitefully use you. Read Matthew 5:44.

Empowerment 41

"Action is the constant trial of faith. It's easy to be a believer. It's more difficult to live what we say we believe"
-Lance Watson

I confessed that I love the Lord, but my lifestyle said otherwise. I confessed that I love Jesus but my heart was far from him. Most people admit that they are sinner, which we all are, but the ones who are saved, are just sinners saved by grace, but no one admits to being a sinner faking to be a Christian, but we have more people posing as Christians and have never given their life to Christ. We have been taught how to fake it until we make, trained in the routine of ritual living. Living what you believe takes discipline, but most of all it takes Christ in you.

Empowerment 42

"Limitations are invisible barriers that intimidate imagination paralyzed thinking and shuts down the creative process causing you to accept the present state as the apex or "pinnacle" of what is possible."

-T.D. Jakes

"I can't" should not be in our vocabulary. We have seen people who have had less than we have accomplished things that were never imagined. Limitations are the enemy that constantly talks into your ear that you cannot do something because of: your race, background, height, education etc… The sky is the limit. The only person can limit you, is yourself! You have to constantly tell yourself that you refuse to accept anything that stands against you and your goal. Everything will try to come up against you, but you must make up in your mind like Paul did in Roman. Paul made up in his mind that he refused to let anything get in the way of him and his God. Read Romans 8:35-39

Empowerment 43

"If it's meant for you, you will never have to beg for it. You never have to sacrifice your dignity for your destiny."
-Unknown

When it's your time and you are walking in your purpose, things began to fall into place. Your provision is already in place. You do not have to compromise yourself or your dignity to fulfill your destiny. David said in Psalms 23 the Lord is my Shepard, I shall not want. Read Psalms 23

Empowerment 44

"God makes an investment in us NOW based on what God sees happening with us in the FUTURE."

-Lance Watson

God knew us before you were in your mother's womb. He did not decide to call you, once you get yourself together, because if that was the case we would have never been called, but he called us according to the purpose he had intended for us. God calls you what you are and not what you think you are. Abram=Abraham, father of many nations, Simeon=Peter, a rock. These men did not appear to be what God was calling them, but eventually they became what God had already spoken over their lives, regardless of their faults, failures, doubts and fears.

Empowerment 45

"Nobody can give you what you don't want"
-Unknown

Nobody can give you what you do not want. This is such a true statement. Christ died for the entire world, and paid the ultimate price for our sins. Salvation is free, and heaven is to gain and no one has to go to hell, which was created for Satan and his angels, but Jesus cannot give you something that you do not want. By refusing salvation you accept the sin that you are in, as well as the end result of it, death and hell. Nobody in their right mind wants to go to hell but, they are not doing anything to keep from going. The lake of fire is eternal separation from God, never to experience his love again. Do not let your chance pass you by.

Empowerment 46

"Sometimes we can be loyal to the wrong things"
-Unknown

We have all played the fool of being loyal to the wrong thing(s), but we could not be loyal to the things that matter. It's amazing that what we should have been loyal too, we were not, but the things we should have avoided, that is what we were loyal too. Do not be tricked into being loyal to something that is not worthy of your loyalty or time.

Empowerment 47

"To err is human, to forgive divine."

-Alexander Pope

As long as I am in human form, I will not always get it right, but through wisdom I will be able to notice the era of my ways and have the opportunity to make it right. But to forgive, that is a gift from God that enables me to look past another person's fault and forgive them. Forgiveness is an act of kindness that you receive, even when you are at fault or guilty of all the charges. But forgiveness says drop the charges and let him/her go. Go in peace and sin no more.

Empowerment 48

"We can worship God imperfectly, but we cannot worship him insincerely"

-Rick Warren

We must find a way to perfect our worship, we have done it collectively for so long that we are able to hide in the crowd, but we need to worship God individually and not just at church either. God inhabits the praise of his people. When we come to God we must realize that we do not have to be perfect, but we cannot worship God insincerely. Perfection is not required but sincerity is. We must love the Lord with all of our heart, soul, mind and strength.

Empowerment 49

"When words are released out of your mouth it gives that thing permission to exist in your life"
-Cindy Trimm

When your words are released out of your mouth, you give that thing which you have spoken, power to exist. The bible declares that life and death are in the power of the tongue. Choose your words carefully, the enemy knows that you possess that kind of power, but we have yet to recognize our full potential, so he gets us to speak things against ourselves and each other. Speak life into yourself and others.

Empowerment 50

"As we grow upward, we need to grow downward as well. We need strong roots and good foundation"
-C.D. Walker

Growing depends on the roots, and a good foundation. The roots must be able to reach the resources that are deep in the time of a drought, because when there is no water on top, it must be able to reach the water below. A solid foundation provides the stability of the structure. A foundation must be formed. Your growth will depend greatly on the foundation that you have laid. Read Matthew 7:24-27

Empowerment 51

"Everybody comes with baggage....find somebody who loves you enough to help you unpack."

-Jamal Bryant

Baggage is a part of life. We all have some. The key to lighting your load is to find someone that loves you enough to help you deal with the stuff you have been carrying around for so long. We carry stuff we do not deal with or confront. We have subconsciously decided that it is better to carry the stuff we do not want and deal with it, then unpack. Sure it might stink, but a person that loves you and care about you will look past the smell and help you deal with the stuff that has been locked away. It is time to unpack.

Empowerment 52

"If you are working on something exciting that you really care about, you don't have to be pushed. The vision pulls you"

-Steve Jobs

Often times we have to be probed and pushed to do something, but when we have vision, it ignites a fire within us. Vision pulls you even when you are not thinking about it; it becomes a part of you. Vision wakes up the creativity inside of you that you never knew you had. Vision transcends all barriers and limitations. Vision gives hope, even when the situation seems hopeless. Read Habakkuk 2:2-3

Be Bold, Empower, Impact and Leave a Trail of Change Behind

Notes

How have this helped you?

_____

_____
_____
_____
_____
_____
_____
_____
_____
_____
_____
_____

How can you help someone else?

_____
_____
_____
_____
_____
_____
_____
_____
_____
_____
_____
_____
_____

Contact Information

c.d.walkerministries@gmail.com

Twitter: CClenta

Facebook: clenta.walker

RP Enterprise Publishing

25670 Fairview Ave

Hemet, CA 92544

951-927-8042

www.rpenterpriseinc.webs.com

www.ingramcontent.com/pod-product-compliance
Lightning Source LLC
Chambersburg PA
CBHW071431040426
42445CB00012BA/1342